MW00377759

A Bob Jones Book

Feeling The Spirit
By Bob Jones author of

No Empty Spaces

The Fire Within

From The Heart

Allowing Abundance

Practising Presence

Feeling The Spirit

Feeling The Spirit is a fresh and modern approach to understanding ageless ancient questions as to who we are, why we are here, and what life is really all about. A refreshing new take on various ways to look within and reconnect to the source of All That Is, to reaffirm and remember our divine birthright, that is to be in a constant connection to spirit, and to really truly be conscious of our ability to Feel The Spirit Within.

Table Of Contents

Bob Jones

Feeling The Spirit

Feeling The Spirit is a modern and contemporary look into an ancient and age old phenomenon of feeling the spirit. What does it mean? How does it feel? Do people really actually become full of the spirit, and able to perform miracles, cure ills, or levitate through the air? What is meant by the word spirit? Through its pages, this book will delve into these mysteries and explore new ways of understanding and learning about what these terms mean and lay reference to. Spirit, God, Source, the Creator, Chi, Prana, Life force, the many ways that humanity has developed to describe the indescribable is a sign of our Infinite imaginations and desire to create.

Bob Jones

Feeling The Spirit

Part One: Knowing The Unknowable

Chapter One

Everything under the sun has been given a name by man, given a description and conception of what we ourselves believe it to be. A name is not what something is, by labelling and defining something, we are not creating it, and controlling it. The only thing that man can control that way is his own perception of a thing. How he himself thinks of it. It's inherent rightness or wrongness, it's worth, value, and place in the world. But by dong so, we take ourselves further and further away from the truth, from what is actually real.

Too often in this modern world of ours we can lose our connection to our inner most core, what makes us who we are, our spirit. Man is not created to be constantly immersed in machinery, googling, tweeting, making status updates. This slow but relentless encroachment upon our day to day life's and entire world by technology and computers has been going on for a few decades now, but since the 2000s rapidly increasing at a pace that is both mind blowing and frightening at the same time.

Years and years ago, when our brother once walked the earth, and lived amongst men, there was no such thing as a computer. There wasn't any TVs, radios, or other such modern distractions that take us away from looking in and discovering our fathers presence for ourselves. Even though there was corruption and illness back then, one thing the people didn't have to deal with is the constant drain of energy that modern man does from technology.

How much time is there left in the day to meditate and contemplate your vey existence when from morning to night we are expected to participate in an endless stream of digital communication. Revealing aspects of our life's to strangers and following other people's as if it was a real life soap opera. The person always on call for their job, the employee never taking time off and always saying yes to over time. The business man who checks his emails 50 times a day never wanting to miss out on a deal, or the actress with her phone glued to her ear waiting for that call from her agent. Even the young with no other commitments, who are fully committed to social media, tweeting more than they talk, and updating their Facebook statuses more regularly than they go and visit their grandparents or read a actual book.

Humanity seems to have got lost and forgotten about the most important important thing, the one thing that truly separates us from all the other animals and life forms on this planet, and that is our own innate connection to spirit. The invisible bond that stretches from our physical forms here on earth all the way up to the Heavenly Father up in Heaven.

Chapter Two

Man is born able to feel the spirit of the Holy Ghost and it is something that is hard wired inside us. When we were created in the image of God all those years ago, it means that not just out physical bodies, but our spirits, which when we truly look within and find out who we really are we find out that there is only one spirit, the one true light that is within me and within every single human being who walks the earth.

Regardless of religious beliefs, country of origin, or what colour or sex we are, we all have the same connection to God inside of us. It is not something that we have to earn through service, a lifetime of work, or something that we can learn and acquire through studying and studying scripture. It is just there. Always has been and always will be. No one can take it away from you, and no actions that you can perform will be able to block this innate connection to the divine.

When we get back down to basics, and think of who we are, and why we are here, it will click into place and start to make sense. We are first and foremost human beings who were created in the image and likeness of God. Full of the same love and knowledge of He who created the earth and with the same guiding light deep down inside of us. From the day we are born until the very day we die, it us our duty to look within and find that spark of the divine within and do all we can to fan it's flames and help it to grow. The brighter our own God light, the more we will understand and be able to help others to see their light too.

We are here to spread the light of God outwards from ourselves to all we come into contact with, to feed our connection to spirit and nurture and nourish it, until we feel connected to The All That Is, all the time. The greater your connection, the greatest will be your earthly rewards. When things don't seem to be working out how you planned, or everything seems to be going wrong in your life, take some time out, look within, maybe the connection to spirit that you had has waned and weakened, which means that it is the perfect time to do what you can to reignite that flame.

The most influential people who leave an indelible mark on the world, long after they have left the earth and gone back to the source, are more often than not, those with a strong innate connection to our Father, a connection to spirit that they have had throughout their life's. All the things that can be thought of and created, already have been in Heaven. The answers to any question that man could ask, or the blueprints for the next great invention that will make life easier for people on earth. The melodies to the most beautiful songs that we could imagine, all that and much more is floating in the ether in Heaven. Nothing under the sun has not been already thought of by Him. Do you not think that when God created man and the world, that it was not an complete creation, where everything that we could ever need has already been thought of?

Looking back over the history books, we will see for ourselves, that the periods of mans greatest achievements, times when he has created enduring monuments, and legacies that last for millennia that he had a very strong connection to spirit. The more connected and inline with our fathers will that we are, the more harmonious and free flowing life here on earth will be.

The greatest thing that separates Jesus the man from me and you, is simple and straightforward. He had a very strong, uninterrupted connection to his Father, the Holy Spirit. From the moment he woke up in the morning, until the time he laid his head down to sleep Jesus's connection to spirit never wavered. When all around him were lost and confused and didn't know the right thing to do, He did.Just by quieting his outer mind and looking within he had all the answers, and knew exactly what to do. When you put your faith and trust in the spirit, it will show you the way forward.

Part Two: Look Within Or Go Without, The Battle Against The Modern Onslaught Of Technology

Chapter Three

Which brings me back to today and the modern world that we are living in. It seems as if, every year, new ways are created and thought up, of taking humanity's focus further and further away from the truth of the world, and what it truly real, which is spirit.

Television is a box that we plug into the electrical socket, turn on and sit and watch, for many of us for hours and hours on end. It has no spiritual value. We can see pretty pictures, hear nice sounds, but it is just a distraction from what is real, and an illusion to keep us constantly entertained and absorbed, with no time left to look within and nurture our own innate connection to the divine. From the advent of radio and television onwards to the Internet and social media. Constant streaming of information 24 hours a day.

In a world where everyone is sharing everything online, their personal information, feelings, what they like and dislike, but no one is truly being themselves, and just trying to put on the face that they see others wearing so that they can fit in and be like them too. If we think for a moment of all the different many ways that have been created to distract humanity, get them online and away from the real world, it makes it seem as if it is a deliberate act, a conscious decision to drive us away from what's real and true, and lure us into a false sense of security that all is well in this imaginary digital world of make belief, where everyone is beautiful and everything is ok all of the time.

For even the Pope himself to be on social media and tweeting his thoughts to the world, it is a very worrying sign indeed. It will get to a point in the not to far future, were we all have to be constantly logged on and connected to the Internet in order to survive and live in the world. But, for that to happen. Who would be left on earth that are still connected to Our Heavenly Father, who have held onto and maintained their connection to sprit.

The constant onslaught of technology, gaining a firmer grip in our life's on a daily basis, is truly frightening. The speed in which TVs have become smarter, the Internet faster, and phones like computers, is astounding. Each year the levels of new digital equipment available grows by leaps and bounds, to where nearly every aspect of our life's, are being enhanced by computers and the free will we once had to make decisions and choose for ourselves, is slowly being taken away from us, until we are informed what our next step should be by Google, or Amazon.

The more we allow our focus to be drawn outwards and away from ourselves, the more we will lose our connection to spirit, and our sense and understanding of the inherent divinity within. Each time we become addicted to the latest bit of new technology, we lose a sense of ourselves and start to worship and admire the inanimate, over the real flesh and blood all around us. It's almost as if it has all been designed this way, to take mankind further and further away from the source, until he has been cast out, wondering aimlessly around the earth, constantly worshipping false idols, giving their power away to lifeless machines and elevating technology to the lofty position where only our father should be.

Part Three: Finding Our Way Back To Source

Chapter Four

Everything that takes your mind and energy away from yourself and stops you from connecting to the spirit within, is taking you further and further away from Heaven. When the earth was created, God thought to give us everything that we could ever need. An endless abundance of supply, so that our life's would be free from worry and our time could be spent in worship and admiration of Him. From the foods that we need to eat to survive, to the water we need to drink and bathe vin.It is all here, and always has been. Like the sun shining down from the heavens, giving us light and allowing life to grow and flourish, He thought of everything that we could ever need.

To wake up and see a beautiful sunrise, watching it slowly come up over the horizon is a sight to see and more than satisfying. To see the full moon in the night sky, and all underneath it illuminated by its heavenly glow. Lightening streaking through a dark and stormy sky, followed by a earth shattering primal clap of intense thunder, is a spine tingling experience. The sights and sounds of nature that God created for and on behalf of man, are of such magnitude and sheer brilliance, that no technological invention, or electronic device such as a television, radio, or laser display, could ever come anywhere near competing with it and being on the same level of experience.

Everything that man can create and conceive of, is but a sheer imitation of the great works of God. To invent and design devices that can aide and help our experience here on earth, are what mankind feels is his greatest achievement, when it reality, it is our ultimate fall from grace, and fastest means of taking us away from our own mate connection to spirit, which is the light of divinity deep down inside each of us.

We witness in these modern times, men who are part of the technological takeover, helping bring forth new ways to distract his fellow man, and take his focus away from himself, and absorbed by the illusionary, false idols of the Internet, reap unimaginable rewards. People who are literary rewarded with billions of dollars, for the fact that they was successful at taking humanity further away from source, and closer and closer to a world that is ruled by lifeless, Godless, machines. When at the same time, those who are out there trying to help people to look within, and re connect to the divinity and light that is there, constantly attacked, abused, and robbed of their dignity, finances, and everything else, by a society that doesn't want to admit about the elephant in the room.

Connection to source, and feeling the spirit within are basic and vital necessities for a healthy, grounded life for all human beings. Like a device which is unplugged from its source the electrical socket, we will cease to function and maintain our full capabilities if we lose the connection to our own source of power, which is being in tune, in touch, and able to fully focus on feeling the spirit within.

All the answers to all the questions we could ever ask, the love, warmth and compassion we have been searching for. The cure for whatever ails us, or makes us feel sick. Needless operations that only really make things worse, not better, could be prevented if people took the time to allow theirselves to be healed internally, from having a greater understanding, and connection to the spirit within. How can we ever hear the voice of God whisper in our ear with the answer to our prayers, if we are constantly distracted by the latest song on iTunes or Spotify, absorbed by the latest blockbuster from Hollywood, or addicted to the new social media craze?

Chapter Five

When we look at life as being about us and God, and the sense of love, compassion, understanding and connection that we feel to His spirit within us, all else becomes a distraction, which is what it is. The truth of the matter is that we are agents of the divine, to act out His will here on earth, but when our focus is taken away from what's within, and we start giving our power away and worshiping what's outside of ourselves, the man made false idols of technology, what will are we channeling? For it is surely not Gods. Pause and think for a moment the next time before you start preaching about the latest iphone, or handheld gadget that's been released, how it's making your life better and how you couldn't live without it. There should be only one thing that any one of us simply can't live without, and that's our connection to the spirit within. Once we are filled with that divine light, and fully connected to the source of All That Is, we already have everything we could possibly need, for when we are at one with Him, we are at one with everything.

There is so much noise in the modern world that man is living in, that it is near on impossible for him to be able to listen to his intuition and the still quiet voice that is within. Like a walk though a maze with no idea where you are going, we walk aimlessly and blindly through life, drawn ever forwards by the brightest lights, or loudest sounds, not having an idea of our end destination, only hoping that it is as good and as satisfying as we are led to believe. All who seek, will in the end find, but the constant need for instant gratification pushed on us by the adverts and slogans in the media and public domain, draw us away from ever thinking that there is anything to seek on the inside, when outside everyone looks so happy, and everything so sparkly and nice.

Like an upside down world, where what people believe and take for granted to be real is only an illusion and the real and true world, invisible to the eye, but often understood and felt by the heart. We are living on a planet on the earthly plane, utilising and contained within physical forms, in order to experience fully earthly reality and immerse ourselves in the material world. But we are more than that and so is the world. Everything that you can see and touch has behind and through it an energy. That same force that causes plants to push up through the ground and seek the light, for the birds to be able to sing and fly, the force that create waves, earthquakes, and volcanic eruptions, flows through us and is what gives us our life force whilst here, an innate connection to nature and Mother Earth.

That's something we inherently have and feel all the time, whether we know it or not. But the connection to source, feeling the spirit within, is something need to maintain and nurture. To look after ourselves and our minds, to keep the way paced clear for the spirit to flow through us. The greatest difference between man and beast, is that man is able to consciously develop this spiritual connection to the divine, by practise, right living, and a faith that he can do so, create a strong and sustained constant connection to the source of The All That Is, which is to be living from a place of feeling the spirit within all the time. To be immersed in the divinity within, and able to share that light and healing knowledge not only with ourselves, healing our own ills, but with others too, giving hope to those without and encouraging others to look within so they too can feel the spirit, and make all as it should be.

It is our struggle to let go of the material illusion and reconnect to the spirit within that makes us human and it's through the trying, failing, and trying again, that we are rewarded with faith, by the innate knowing that it is possible, that others have achieved what we have set out to do, certain from the fleeting glimpses of unconditional love that we have felt with our own hearts during those rare moments of truly feeling the spirit within.

Part Four: Unplug To Reconnect

Chapter Five

If we all took a moment to truly think about it, and take in the enormity of what has been said here, we would come to the realisation that there is absolutely nothing that we have to do, achieve, or gain, to ignite that spark, and discover our own connection to the spirit within, The All That Is. It is what we have to not do, and let go of. To release and cast aside. To go away from the illusion of the outer physical world, even for a few moments, will nourish and nurture your soul. To be able to block out the constant noise, colours, and mental stimulation, to find quiet, calm, peace and stillness.

Through mediation and learning to truly quiet the mind and let go of all outside distractions we can begin to re find that connection.With the use of sounds to take away other mental chatter, and to find somewhere where you can be at peace with the stillness that is already all around us, when we take the time to listen, we find it there.

Things such as flotation tanks are great beneficial creations, where a person can lay fully immersed in salty water, floating in the body temperature saline mixture in complete darkness and silence, it's the perfect thing for modern day man to reconnect and learn to discover their innate connection to source, for in the stillness and silence, we find out that we are all part of the same thing, the one light that is within everything, The All That Is, God.

Throughout the many millennia, philosophy's, ways of living and being a part of the world, have changed and developed, varying immensely throughout the ages. From ancient times of hunter gathering, to Ancient Greece and Egypt with their complex religions and various forms of art, to medieval times of knights and castles, onwards to the Industrial Age of steam and coal, to the modern age of technology, with all of its constantly upgrading smartphones and tablets, faster and faster internet connection and instant access to all the information we want when we want it. One thing that has remained the same, and has always been there, no matter what the age, or the current stage of development humanity has reached, is that overwhelming, never ending, internal desire to find the light that we know is there and re connect with it, to find the source, and once again be able to feel the sprit.

We all know on a subconscious level, that we are spirits inside our physical forms, more than meets the eye, we feel each other's spiritual energy on a daily basis through the interaction that we have with other people. Be it uplifting, depressing, or even energising and fast or slow. It's one of the first things that we take in about a person, from the time we meet there is an instant knowing of whether you like their energy and are drawn to it, or if you don't like it at all, and instead feel repelled and want to be nowhere near it, or them. Instant feelings of trust and faith in a person and who they are, are a natural aspect of human life, how many times have we all met someone for the first time and thought straight away that we would happily put our life's in their hands?

Chapter Six

Trust, is one of the first things we need to develop and truly comprehend, before we can set out upon the path of being able to feel the spirit within. To learn once again to let go of any worries, fears, or uncertainties of how life is or how we think it should be. To trust in the natural simplicity of life, that we are here, right now, at this very moment alive and here on a beautiful planet called Earth. Life is here, right here and right now, and there is absolutely nothing that we or anyone else can do to influence its course. Life has found a way here, from amongst the billions of planets in the countless other solar systems, through adversity, obstacle, and sheer impossibility, it has, and it will always find its way.

Trust in the fact that your journey is yours alone, and wherever it is that you currently find yourself, is in fact, exactly where you need to be. Believe wholeheartedly that the people that you know, and have in your life, are there for a reason and are supposed to be there. Trust in the magic and mystery of the universe, that it has all been thought up in the infinite, immense mind of Him, and that every little thing, is how He wants it to be. By developing trust, in ourselves, life, and the world around us, it will lead us onto faith, which is the natural next step, from trusting, to without any form of uncertainty, knowing without a shadow of a doubt. Trust, can be taught, developed, nurtured in order to help it grow, but faith, can only grow naturally from within.

Through real, genuine, total faith, what was once impossible, becomes possible, and where before no way excited, a way will be made clear. The greatest thing we can have on our side against the onslaught of falsehoods, illusions, and destructive push of technology, is faith. It's something invisible, it can't been seen, it's silent and can't be heard. But it can be felt, and nothing is as powerful a force, as the faith of someone who knows he is feeling the spirit, for it The All That Is, by its very nature is all that is, and by connecting to it, you become connected to everything.

Faith as small as a mustard seed can move mountains as the proverb goes, this is an expressing of the interconnectedness of all life, of light that animates and sustains nature and the animal world, the same force that cause the winds to blow and the seeds to sprout and grow. This is inside us as it is in all life, when we learn to feel the spirit within, which is the same spirit that is within everything we are a part of the whole, the All That Is. And a part can control another part of the same body, and having faith and feeling of the spirit enables us to control our destiny by control if and how the physical world affects us. If we only knew the countless times that are lives have been saved and tragedy averted, through the sheer power and force of our own inherent faith that things would work out and everything would be OK.

A person connected and I tune with the feeling of the spirit within is lit up spiritually though the light of our Heavenly Father and full of an endless supply of universal love and divine grace. It is what we were born to aspire to, a deeper and deeper, more constant non stop uninterrupted connection to the source, whilst having abundant, harmonious, life's here in the physical world. To have one foot in heaven and one foot on earth as such. It's by being the bridge of this connection between the higher and lower worlds, that we allow our dreams to manifest. By believing first in what we can't see, we make the room in this reality for it to actually happen and come to pass. Everything is a form of energy, and the greater the believe and faith in an outcome, the more likely it is to happen, by sheer force of will power and uninterrupted focus of energy.

Creation is a natural gift that all humans are capable of, the vast majority, only blindly, and unconsciously. To be alive is to be creating, to exist requires imagination and a desire to be a part of something that you have some control over. The more we are conscious in our creation, the greater the depth and understanding within us that through our thoughts, words, and feelings, let alone our very actions that we take using our physical bodies that we are creating our life experience, day by day, from one moment to the next. It enables us to flex that inner internal muscle of creation and develop it until it becomes strong through use, and easier to access and use whenever we consciously choose to do so.

Chapter Seven

The more we are in control of our own destiny, the simple the path becomes to be in a position to make our dreams come true. We are here to live out our dreams, those lofty fantasies where everything is how we would like it to be, aren't just idle day dreams, or ideas that are impossible to create. We dream and hope and pray for a better world, because it is possible. The fact that we have an idea of how we would like it to be, should give us the courage and faith that that same very world, where all is how it should be, is right here and right now in front of us, that it always has been and always be, like a world without end. The question is, why are we not there? Why are we not in that place where dreams come true, and we all have the happy ever after we hope for? The answer lies within ourselves, for it is humanity that distances itself from the ultimate reality, and too often blocks it's divine birthright of peaceful and harmonious living, by the sheer force of the energy or expectation. What we allow to come into our lives, what we are able to accept and believe is how it should be, is normally exactly the way that it is.

Man has a tendency to doubt how own worth, and what he is capable of. Finding it easier to give their power away to leaders outside themselves, to others who will do the work needed, leaving it up to anyone apart from we ourselves, as to how the world should be. It's simpler to listen to rules, and follow regulations, than to really spend the time getting to know oneself, who we really are inside, and what we are about. To take the time away from the bright lights and loud noises of the modern world, and delve into the internal world, full of magic, mystery and wonder that lies deep down inside us, buried far within.

For in the stillness and silence that lies within man, the unfathomable depths, of calm, peace, tranquilly that are at the heart of not just us, but all of life, we find the source, the place where we all come from, and where we will all return. There is a place without beginning and without end, a time, that has always been and always will be, when we know ourselves, on a deep and real level, we will come to learn, that the depths of our being, is rooted in that place, and we find the stillness within, and be centred and aligned with that, we are connected and at one with everything.

The more we focus on the eternal aspects of ourselves the more fluid will be our journey through the physical world, and the transient reality of the here and now. To come from a place of understanding the wider picture, and being aware of the dual aspect of life, the push and the pull, the fast and the slow, the loud and the quiet, we see first hand for ourselves, that the intent of all life is inherently the same. It's a striving to grow, to live, to seek its blueprint for structure and potential. By serving another, we also serve ourselves, by helping any other form of life, we are also helping Him. It should be the norm for us to look to another, and see who we are through them. To take in the outside world or the natural world, and see reflected in its sights, our own inertial struggles, successes, and who we are.

Part Five: The Reflection Of Reality

Once we connect to the source of The All That Is and have a deep understanding of the feeling of spirit, to feel the light that we are inside and be able to consciously express that, through our thoughts, words, actions, then we can step up into the ultimate reality, where all of our dreams come true, and the billions of prayers for peace have already been answered. To have one foot upon heaven and the other here on earth is mans destiny. When we were crated in our fathers likeness, to be an aspect of Him, on a minute scale, He gave us everything we would need. Nothing was left to chance or circumstance, and the things that He wanted us to have, were created alongside us.

Open your eyes, and take in a deep breathe. Think for a moment of the times in your life where you were certain that something was right for you, and would be a great benefit to you and all those around you too. When you absolutely knew that it had to come to pass. It did didn't it?! When we acknowledge how powerful we are, how far our energy extends outwards from ourselves, and interacts with everything else around it, we come to understand that when we are truly in alignment with Him, and what He wants, then it has to happen. It's not a question of hoping, praying, or believing, it's about developing the confidence in ones self, and our Father up in heaven, that He is as real as us, come to know when you feel His presence around you, inside you, and trust that when you know by the sheer act of your faith, that it is knowledge more true and sound than any other. It's through knowing, that we can tear apart the veil of illusion separating us from the ultimate reality, and walk through into that world we always dreamed of, the place we kind of remember, but seem to have forgotten was even there in the first place.

Chapter Eight

We are the ones who block the flow of our own divine birthright of natural abundance and a rich and fulfilled life, by not believing it is possible, that are dreams are unobtainable and not having faith in Him, that through him all things are possible. Everything is energy. The greater the internal block of our own from being able to receive the external things flowing to us, the less and less we will have and experience, being unable to receive through a closed looped circuit. We cut ourselves off from the great supply all around us by, not knowing, not having faith that it is there and only believing in the small fraction of existence that we can see with our own two physical eyes.

Open your heart, open your mind, open your understanding to the reality that all is well, has been well, and always will be well. Go deep within where you come to feel for yourself that innate inner connection to Him, where you start to genuinely feel the spirit within, and all will be well. Let your own desires, intertwine, and mingle with His, let your actions and words, flow from that deep place of understanding within, where we are all one, and everything we do is in praise of Him. Like the birds singing in the trees, the butterfly's flapping its wings, all of nature is in rapturous joy at being alive and able to express its love for itself, each other, the very life force itself that animates them and us too.

We are here to be happy, free, to take the greatest possible pleasure from each and every moment. To live the life's that we have always dreamed of, and love the love we always had hoped and believed to be possible and true. Mankind should be the ultimate expression of divinity on earth, a custodian, ambassador and effortless representation of His will. To be anything other is to deny who we are and what we are about. To shut out the whispers of our soul, and burry our heads in the sand, deeply aware, but unable, or just in denial of the natural birthright of our spiritual heritage. To deny the truth, to block the flow of inherent abundance is our greatest challenge we are facing, and something we have become so used to doing, that for the vast majority, the energy of their belief in its impossibility makes it impossible for them to realise.

Chapter Nine

Feeling the spirit on a constant basis, maintaining a consistent connection to source, to The All That is is the goal of mankind, and a vital necessity for its survival, and future here on planet earth. To be who and what we came here to be, is why we are here. It's not to learn, do or be anything other than that in which we are, if we could only therefore just be it. Be us, be ourselves, be connected to the one true, Holy Spirit within, and be part of everything. Let the spirit flow freely through our thoughts, words, and actions, let His love for life, and our love for Him, be the guiding force behind every step we take or word we speak.

The more that we walk along our journey in faith, that all will be well, that all of our dreams are possible as all things are possible through Him and the spirit that dwells deep down inside all of us. The more that it will be well, and our dreams will come true. Slowly, like a bear eking from its hibernation, we can start to really come alive, and utilise everything that has always been available to us, by the power of the spiritual force of our faith, knowingness.

As we begin to cement on connection to our centre and feeling the spirit on a constant basis, we enlarge and strength the bond between us, and everything else around us. By going within, and discovering the depths, and magnitude of our own souls, we touch upon and begins to understand and have empathy for others, as at our inner most core, we are all the same light that is connected to the source, we are all an aspect of everything.

Disharmony in our life's and affairs becomes impossible for when we find the calm, peaceful, harmonious place within, all our outer experiences will reflect that, for as above, so below, and vice versa.

The less we dwell upon the preconceived perceptions that are constantly pushed upOn us on a non stop daily basis, and focus on nature, the world around us, the stars, ourselves, and put more trust in what we can feel, not just what we can see. Then we will start to life those life's that we have always imagined and dreamed about. If you are constantly being told what is possible and what is not, the reality that you live in will become the one that you have been consistently told to believe in. Thoughts are powerful things, the more you give them away to things that you are told you need and want, the less control you will have to be able to use them to go out there and achieve your very goals and aspirations.

Listen to the quiet, focus upon the internal stillness and calm. Learn to let go of other factors pulling to you this way, or pushing you that way, remember that all is well, has always been well, and will always be well, know it in your heart, and have faith in Him, that your life will be a reflection of His will on earth. Don't doubt your own innate power to connect to the divine within and to come from there, to be who you came here to be, who we all did. Then watch you life change. . . .

Part Six: To Know Thyself

Chapter Ten

Through self knowledge and an understanding of who we are and why we are here, all ties that bind us to the illusions of the physical world are cut and naturally will fall away. By a knowingness of our own innate connection to source, all obstacles, and perceived difficulties fade away. Everything, doesn't want to consciously harm anything, for to do so would be to harm itself, for anything is truly everything and everything anything on a deeper sub atomic spiritual level. When we know this, not just intellectually but instinctively, intuitively, on a real basic level, the fear of loss and separation disappears, and a knowingness, a faith, that anything is possible becomes evident, and the knowledge, faith, it does.

The evolution of humanity, from the ancient times of Egypt and Greece, to Medieval, and Renaissance onwards and upwards to the modern era through the swinging sixties, to the creativity and expression of the nineties, have always been leaning towards one thing. Self knowledge, man has been yearning, seeking, trying ever so hard to really get to know himself, who he is, what he is, why he is here, and through all different forms or media and expression available to him, showing and sharing his ideas, and wanting to experience and see, others ideas and concepts to those age old questions. Dress it up as entertainment, art, science, it all leads and points to the same thing. To know the truth of ourselves, to seek a knowledge that cannot be taught, but can only be discovered and unlearned, finally accepted and understood from coming to a deep realisation from within.

Listening to our own intuition and feeling the pull of the spirit within are not what we are taught to do, or even expected to understand. Society structured to always have the Individual seeking outside help and guidance, to look to other sources to gain the things that they want and need, when all along the answer to all the questions we have and the place where everything is there that we need, is and has been inside of us. The world has been too focused on what's outside, and this has what has caused us to lose our way. It is time to remember, to recall who we are, what we are about, and that deep down inside each of us, we are connected to The Source, to The All That Is, and through that internal connection we are also connected to everything.

Part Seven: Remembering Who We Really Are

Chapter Eleven

Instead of learning, being taught by other outside sources who we are, we need to start to look within, and remember what we already know, to unlearn the falsehoods of our current reality that are ingrained in our consciousness and to reveal the true understanding that lies in the depth of our souls, our own innate connection to the source of everything, and the feeling of the spirit that is within.

We feel on a deep and real level the huge immensity of our souls, our spirits, the light that is inside each and everyone of us. We know that we are part of the same spirit that is inside of everything, we just need to remember and truly trust what we do indeed already know. By having faith in things unseen we open up reality to be ready and able to receive them, like making room in our house for a long awaited guest, we need to make room in our hearts and our world, for all of the things we truly want to happen, by believing in them, and developing an innate knowingness of their very existence and probability that they will happen and come to pass. It's the trust in the unknowable that gives it the energy and power to actually become knowable in the first place.

From knowing that all we need is already here, and that in trusting our own intuition and the feelings we get when we know we are right and walking along the path we are supposed to, we gain a power that can and does control our outer reality. Day by day, the more we focus on the internal and eternal aspects of ourselves, the more we will be able to realise these in our day to day, physical life's. To bring forth who we really are into the world, and therefore creating the world that we have always wanted to live in.

Man has to come to know himself in a real and profound way, for all of the riches of heaven to be made available to him. To have the peace we have for millennia prayed and hoped for, we need to look deep inside of ourselves, to discover its presence there inside of us, and ground our being in the reality of that peace, to come from there, to live it, to be it, and to bring it forth form inside of us, our into the wonder physical world. We are the heroes that we have been seeking, the leaders to lead the way, and the saviour of ourselves. The key to the greatest mysteries, the answers to every question under the sun, is who we are and what we are, for we are truly everything. Love each other as you would love yourself and you will on the path to truth, for we are each other. Deep down we are all the same, a small fraction of the one light, the spirit of God, the source of everything, and when we begin to be able to feel the spirit, to know ourselves, we become the unifying factor linking the physical world on earth to the spiritual world of Heaven.

Chapter Twelve

The future is not such a far off thing, sometimes we have to look back to see forwards and the greatest things that we will discover and come to realise is are the things that we already knew, but have forgotten. What was once lost, will be found. It is our destiny and innate part of the evolution of mankind to really come to know himself and therefore to know God. To rediscover the light that is within and allow the sprit to flow freely, feeling the spirit and living from that place of truth and understanding all the time. We are here to do His work, and the sooner we cast aside our doubts and our fears as to who we really are, and take ownership of ourselves and the world we are living in, the sooner Thy Will will be done, and we can live a happy, harmonious love filled life of peace on earth.

The real aim of all religions why they were set up in the first place, was to help guide and show mankind a way back to himself, a path to inner reflection and realisation that the source of all life is inside of us, and we in turn are a part of everything. Many different ways to say a similar thing, to illustrate previous examples of others who have rediscovered themselves and become the very thing that they seek. To show is that what they can do, we can do also, and to help push mankind along the way back home through gentle encouragement and simple guidance.

The message has got lost and too much emphasis put on one way or the other to get to the same destination. Saying only one way is the right way, and that by following another, you lose all hope of ever getting there and are a sworn enemy to all those who do. We need to wake up from our long slumber, and come to remember that we are the way. We are the path, the answer, the secret key to everything. It is we ourselves who we pray to, and hope to save us, when we learn to trust the truth of the feeling of spirit within, we will see the light.

Doubt is self created and like a filter through which we see the reality of our life and our world. The illusion lack and limitation that we take for the truth, has blinded us, and kept us from experiencing for ourselves, first hand, the beauty of our ultimate spiritual reality of abundance and free flowing love that is the feeling and realisation of the spirit buried deep within. It's our current perceptions, that define our reality when they all are we can see, as anything else, we force into the realms of improbability due to our total lack of awareness of its sheer possibility.

Fear of anything, is a drain of energy, resources and a block upon the opposite of the thing that is feared. By focusing on the ways and outcomes we don't want to happen, we leave little room for inspiration, guidance from within, as to how to achieve the very things that we do want. The feeling of fear, deflates, lessens, depletes us, as its an opposite feeling of being connected to source, which is uplifting, recharging, and rejuvenating. By trying our backs and focus away from The All That Is, we close the door to its wonders, and majesty entering our life's. By not giving our energy to the task of appreciating the beauty and perfection of life and The Lord we turn our backs on what He has planned for us and blind ourselves to the richness, and wonder of the life that is right here in front of us.

To see and acknowledge the perfection of His creation, is to know thyself and to truly understand that all is one. For the source of everything is what unites us all, and connects us through the different variations of life back to the source of the All That Is.

Feeling The Spirit

The End

Last word: We all have buried deep down inside of us, a real and everlasting connection to the source of everything, The All That Is. Through prayer, mediation, mindfulness and developing a faith in a higher power and that all things are possible through Him, we can live the life's we want and have always dreamed about right here on earth. That is His will, and when we become conscious of our inherent divinity and connection to God, when we truly learn to Feel The Spirit Within, then all that was once deemed impossible becomes possible and the promise of Heaven on Earth can be realised.

Much love and respect to each of you, out there in the world on your own individual journeys back home, sending love, compassion and gratitude for your very existence, let's fight the good fight, become the best possible versions of ourselves that we can, and help each other along the way, knowing that by helping another to see the light, our own becomes brighter, and the sooner they get back home, the sooner we will get there too, as I am You and you are Me, and we are All each other.

One Love.

Yours faithfully Mr Bob Jones 29/12/2016

Made in the USA
Coppell, TX
19 June 2023